Confession of an Immortal Lover

Confession of an
Immortal Lover

IMMORTAL LOVE THAT REFUSES TO DIE

MR. BENOI NAIR

PARTRIDGE
A Penguin Random House Company

To order additional copies of this book, contact
Toll Free 800 101 2657 (Singapore)
Toll Free 1 800 81 7340 (Malaysia)
orders.singapore@partridgepublishing.com

www.partridgepublishing.com/singapore

Brief/ Something about the book

Once in a lifetime everyone falls in love and if your feelings are true, the entire universe conspires in your fairy tale. However, I wish to reflect on the dark part of love and how the pain is equally enjoyable when you have an incomplete story to tell. Yes, it's not poetry or a sonnet but a story that I wish you to experience, especially the youth.

As the title does not suggest, the book is actually a collection of heart written poems that portray honest confession of an 'Immortal Lover'. The words deployed in this book are true feelings garnered in the most beautiful and simple manner, in a language that only a lover can understand. *The book is dedicated to the one who left an imperfect me in this perfect world which still fails to accept me, and to the madness that made me write through these sleepless nights.*

"Some stories remain incomplete… incomplete forever. Writing these stories is an Immortal Lover"

About Me

They say I am a lonesome warrior, who refuses to accept that the war he tries to fight and win was lost long ago. Deep inside I am still a child that carries a dream made of glass, walking carefully in a darksome night, with only fireflies that guide him towards redemption. I hope my simple poems find a pleasant way in to your beautiful hearts and enlighten your soul with the enigma called 'Immortal love'...

Love Untamed...

Feelings leave everything mortal behind and whatever left
behind is not a soul,
It is like being tied by the throat to a barbwire and what lies
ahead is your goal,
Whatever I say comes out as her name,
Rest what remains is a madness that no one can tame,

What love did to me was more than a deed,
Often I wonder if such insanity was ever a need,
Endless love is what it had a name,
All I did was scream at the sky…. For only the creator was
to blame,

Hiding in the dark corners… all the lover did was peek,
His love had no idea what the mad poet and his poems seek,
His sad eyes always had one question framed,
When will she enter his haunted boulevard and when his
madness will be tamed? B~

Ocean and the shore

The ocean longs for the shore,
Have never seen any more beautiful affair,
Like a flower that bends with the breeze,
Leaves time motionless and everything around to freeze,

Their love has beaten the testament of time,
Just like the universe conspiring to show that you've always
been mine,
The heart still longs for your warmth and touch,
Sometimes it stops beating as life has not offered us much,

Even I wish a life like an ocean,
Wander aimlessly and sometimes lie lifeless without motion,
Wonder if we end up just like the moon and stars,
Will our love burn bright or will the time leave its scars,

Grace my life and be the symphony that craves for life,
It's been long playing violin with my wrist and knife,
Soon breathing will also become a monotonous chore,
My hands keep painting incompleteness while the heart
longs for an affair like the ocean and the
shore...

The Mirage

They say she is gone and just a memory,
She was my beautiful poem and the best part of glory,
Life all of a sudden seemed to be a blessing with her,
I had every reason to believe that the mad poet was in love
with a traveller,

She was a mirror whom I could stare endless,
Make sure I had a heart that was not lifeless,
Without her I felt like a forgotten script behind rusty bars,
For once my lonesome sky was studded with stars

It's been ages I have been roaming this realm alone,
I have been pushed, laughed at and agony prone,
Fire in me has died and what's left are some shades of grey,
Wish she would set my soul on fire that fades me away,

I've been lost in her love symphony for ages,
Everyone has left this poet with grief and sympathy as
bandages,
Hold my dreams tightly before they are scattered with the
wind,
Hold my hands tighter for these tears have reduced me to a
warrior that is now blind….B~

Dry Leaf...

The boy is watching the sky as if he is in search for something,
Dry leaf falling all over as stories written in not ink but anything,
He thinks of his dreams and what all happened to them,
Then again he often wondered what these leaf meant and what all was written on them,

These dry leaf were descriptions of his own memories that wished to be burnt,
Every leaf depicting a memory that he cherished and a new lesson he learnt,
He lies with all the dry leaf surrounding him like a forgotten story,
Every fragment of the story depicts a warrior and his lost glory,

What others consider a dream is actually a prayer,
Request to grant love a new life and a last chance to the amateur player,
Grey are the feelings that make the child all human again,
He plays with the leaf as if life will smile at them again,

He awaits someone to come and burn these leaf on a friendly note,
These memories deserve a beautiful death as the boy finds no longer a smiling HOPE....B~

The Lover

I am in search of every other moment where my love looks splendid,
Little did I know it was a rare godly combination, a rare mixture of love n' cuteness blended,
Never in my thoughts did I find you shining so bright,
I don't care even if end up burning my own eyes... You look gorgeous tonight,
Let's search for a moment called love forever,
For the rest of my life I wish to be known as your immortal lover...

I know there might be several others waiting for you to just smile,
I know they would go millions in terms of mile,
Hiding behind all these masks is your lover...waiting for an endless dance,
Pleading for a limitless romance... even-if bestowed with half a chance...
Will be with you even if I have to question the creator,
For the rest of my life I wish to be known as your immortal lover...

Neither did I care for the dress you're wearing,
Nor did I stare at your highlights that are glaring,
It is your eye that drives the sanity out of my life,
A strange obsession dwells inside of me... that wants you to be my wife...
Your memories have been engraved on my mind forever,
For the rest of my life I wish to be known as your immortal lover...

Alcohol

Shiny and elegant seem so lesser world words to me,
Or should I say the grasping beauty doesn't allow anything
to come near me,
Enigma is the only word that comes near,
Its better one stays away if he holds his life very dear,

Staring at the glass glowing is an amusement in itself,
For a moment I feel numb and for a moment god seems
selfless,
They call me mad as I stay in a single state of mind,
They can neither feel the pain nor the journey... for they
ever will be blind,

Have been a mad lover of alcohol all my life,
Time made me treasure this heavenly poison as a noble wife,
Fire that burns within tells me I am alive,
With every heart beat I lose my will to survive,

As I near the end of this majestic charm,
I find myself staring at a starry sky on an abandoned farm,
Alcohol somehow takes me a step closer to her,
Slowly I feel her close to my heart and my imperfect dreams
continues further,

World laughs at the pain when the toxicity fades away,
I find even the moon laughing at my grief as her rhythm
begins to sway,
I see the masks mocking at my misery and the sky starts
burning,

I am left barefoot walking towards oblivion while my feet are still bleeding,

"Often some Love stories are inked in pain…the pain that lasts forever…
It is me who carries this pain as your Immortal Lover…".-
Benoi Nair

When the night comes calling

Hiding behind silently watching his love smile,
Life will again seem kind even if together we walk a mile,
Immortal love has always been an immaculate conception for mankind,
But is there something as immortal as this lover's pride or has time been just kind?

Watching you smile was always a pride within…for I have been your lover since eternity,
I may not be lucky enough to hold your hand…dreaming a life with you has been a penalty,
Wish she could ever touch this pale heart,
And save me from my own memories torn apart,

The heart burns on seeing someone else in your eyes,
The moment you came closer the heart skipped several beats as a price,
Rarely one could understand the level of madness that the lover beholds for you,
A stare into my sad eyes will show you an ocean of emotions not blue,

This tender darkness somehow hides my pain,
Watching you smile gives me the liberation I always wished to obtain,
Since the moment she left tides of time have been crawling,
The lover still waits for the perfect moment when the night comes calling….

Brave heart

Wrote a million times on pages of her eyes,
An affair meant to burn forever but eventually dies,
Angry on himself he sits with a rejected art,
Silence that surrounds him seems like a punishment but still he is a brave heart,

Strange is a bond that sees them miles apart,
Pure is that love that finds shattered dreams in its path,
She left long ago but he still walks with her,
No hand to hold but strives to take the story further,

Wish someone could understand the song that bleeds in silence,
Someone who cherishes his madness without melodious preference,
Waiting for her he still roams in the dark,
They say he is a shattered child smiling with a brave heart,

Once in a lifetime you find a second chance,
Another reason for a prolonged romance,
Storytelling has always been a forgotten art,
Million stories waiting to burn and what remains is one bleeding brave heart... B~

Immortal Thirst...

It's raining outside and it's all wet,
Tears hide with the rain drops and still thirsty is the mad
poet,
If he writes his heart they say it's an ocean of sadness,
Silence that he loves is considered a proof of his madness,

The moon people see is love child of stars,
What shines to the onlookers is more than a legacy of scars,
The poet loved life once like an innocent child,
He used to write feelings and legacies to which they all
smiled,

Poems that people cherish n' admire… to him it's all waste,
He now writes in cold blood ink n' in life he has lost all taste,
Sometimes it hurts deep inside and feels a bit alive,
Every breath seems a new struggle and a new strive,

"They ask me why I don't smile,
I feel so alone when I look back at my story,
The soul is cold with thirst that this mad poet cannot even walk
a mile…"

Ophelian...

In the dark corners of my psychotic heart,
There still exists a corner that desires her,
Life n' instances have always proved like a dart,
Piercing my heart in a place where I still cherish her,

She went and took all the bitter sweet memories,
Still she asks me not to cry,
Weird is the situation as we both miss the lovely mysteries,
Tired is the soul but the heart still wishes to try,

No matter how strong the plea seems to be,
Destiny had a different play in mind,
Story started by the lover was nothing more than just a careless whisper,
Dead was the love and the destiny was now blind,

I wished her always to be the dawn,
While I still remain as dusk,
Dreams ended with one being a pawn,
While the story remains trapped in husk,

Million stories to tell, Million memories to burn….Immortal Hatred ~ Ben

Partners in Pain...

Every glance upon her beautiful face reminds me of how short life is,
With every step that I take holding her I feel even the millennium falling short,
Despite of being an atheist she somehow makes me pray for this time to freeze within this lovely moment,
So let's forget time that flows in vain and be the partners in pain...

I try to see a lover in her which is why I hold her hands tight,
I wish to stay close to her which is why I hold her close to me with my senses uptight,
Joy or pain it doesn't matter all I have is you to share with,
Smile for me as it eases my pain and be with me as a partner in pain...

Each kiss with you I see hope coming back to life,
Wish you could borrow the same hope that dwells between us,
A strange wish to hide you from this incomplete world is I carry,
Life will never be a sinful game... only if you will be my partner in pain,

Life now hangs between you and oblivion,
I walk blindly with no expectations but endless love,
With a promise planted as a kiss,
Will beat even death if it comes as a bane… let's forget this
life and be partners in pain,

"Does love give you a second chance to live?
Don't know…." – Immortal Love-

Salvation

He cannot live without you,
For you may be the reason for his existence,
You wish to remain anonymous to your beloved,
How strange is this persistence?

He is not able to define this relation,
A bond that refuses to name itself,
Is this the moment that they call 'salvation'?
Why don't they ever reveal themselves?

He gave the desired time,
He gave away the distance,
Still his stars do not shine,
He fails to feel her presence,

To live and die for someone you love,
The affair seems so legit,
Imaginations fail to see the daylight of actuality,
It's better to kill it....

Roaming in search of salvation.....Ben~

Unfaithful...

Blood, blood and oceans of blood that I wish to see,
Holding a knife tight in my hand I wish to carve a matinee,
Her eyes still seem so lovely and still so innocent,
Wish the knife slips away for my thoughts are still persistent,

Let me hit her and let me stab her hard,
Pain she has gifted me is infinite and reason I ended as a bard,
Alcohol is no therapy as it fails to curb the pain,
I wish to see her scream as I slowly scratch her bloodless vein,

I kiss her violently as I control the blood lust,
Last goodbye as being a lover I need to be just,
Ending her this way was not the last page of my story,
Only a drop from the ocean of sorrows that easily mask a lover's glory,

Staring at the stars as I lay and smile,
Numbness throughout my body as life will leave me in a while,
Killing her was an obsession that remained a dream,
How could I kill my own first love? And the reason why I cut my own blood stream???

"For my story will be written in blood,
After reading they will shed tears in red,
Feeling my pain they all will scream,
Praying each moment of agony that all this be a bad dream.." –
Searching for love (immortal lover-)

Umbrella...

He knows life will betray him somehow,
He still walks the rain with his umbrella trying to smile anyhow,
May be he doesn't care about a possible tomorrow,
Or maybe he doesn't believe in a time that one cannot borrow,

The life seems a beautiful lady within the umbrella's shade,
This breeze relieves the wounds incurred by life's blade,
The sands of time slip as he feels the wet sand beneath his little feet,
Happy with his umbrella he plays in mud as if there was enough time to beat,

Soon the wet rain will bid the forgotten child a dry farewell,
Even unhitched the gallows of time will refuse to heal his dream as well,
Fades his joyful face as he watches the rain slowly meeting its death,
Stands there holding his umbrella waiting to redeem his timeless debt,
And it goes on...................B~

Let's walk alone....

I walked to the same place again after a while,
As I grew tired and turned to realize I haven't travelled even
a mile,
The thought of her leaving still strikes my mind,
Loving her endlessly has after all left me mad and blind,

Let's walk alone my princess as the world doesn't understand
my pain,
No matter how much I run after them... my efforts still go
in vain,
To them I am just a reflection or a shadow just part of the
dark,
I have to keep failing till the end and lose my spark,

Why did you leave me? For the world is too perfect,
I the grumpy one surrounded by people with intellect,
I still miss the way you made my world smile,
Please let's walk together again even if it's for a while,

Tired of making castles that are meant to be blown,
Let's leave the world again and just walk alone....

Immortal Incompleteness~ B

By chance... Love

By chance I just found her… may be she was broken,
All she does is speak of getting lost,
When a deep stare in her eyes can leave my time frozen,

By chance I fell in love with her… may be she loves me less,
All she does is find ways to ignite a quarrel,
While I still wishto show my love for her will always be limitless,

By chance I saw the light in her eyes… may be she wanted to burn the stars,
All she wants is to hide behind the clouds,
May be she prefers to twinkle like burning buzzards trapped in jars,

By chance I started a new life with her… may be she was meant to be with me,
All she wants is to slow down and be lost,
May be she is yet to see the ocean of love waiting within me,

"Love that was never before… feelings so endless,
May be it's a punishment for being an atheist,
I love her more than my life but she loves me a little less…"—
Yours Immortal Lover-

Sweet Pain

Why do you test me my mistress when you can make me all yours?
You know I stare with dreams in eyes that wish to see the day light,
How can this blind love and this madness go in vain?
When you are adamant on bestowing me with this sweet pain...

I say I have no tears and yet I cry in darkness,
I say I have no anger yet I scratch my broken heart for the last blood,
I still try to hide the marks on my body from time's cane,
Still my mistress is adamant on bestowing me with this sweet pain...

Often I hold your hand tight because I fear distance,
Even though I have you but still this heart prays in silence,
Don't let anger sulk you as your lover can be lame,
Even though this hurts I still like this sweet pain,

My eyes never rest but I never get tired of staring at you,
Shackles of slumber ask redemption but I never get tired to kiss you,
May be she knows I have no one else to blame,
This is why my mistress bestows me with this sweet pain...

Immortal love ~ B

Beautiful Night & Shattered Glasses

Some nights have a beauty of its own or maybe he loves the beauty that night beholds within itself. Night is mysterious with a million secrets entangled in a beautiful manner that can make anyone fall in love with its enigma. Even that night was beautiful when he went to meet this beautiful drunk queen of the night,

There she walked with several dreams falling out of her wings, carefully she picks every step and keeps moving towards a path unknown to her even. Even the silence seems to sing around her lips, such is her elegance. He followed her like a stalker while stared like a lover who lost his pride to a beauty unknown to even the creator. As he walks behind her, he leaves dreams of love made of glasses trailing behind with a hope to pick them later with her. Never ever one has felt endless love for someone who is yet to be his destiny. Then why does life smile when he is with her? Why do questions run around him like mocking wild rabbits? Why he does not wish to live another day without her?

As she stares blankly at the starry sky with questions, he stares at her with eyes full of dreams that of a lovely tomorrow. He wishes to take her in his arms and vanish to a realm that he created for her and her only. An immortal desire to be one with his love ruins his incomplete sleep; somehow his lips wish to get sealed with hers' to protect the secret he has been carrying in his heart from the moment he saw her. As he kneels down, takes her little feet and holds it in his palm and begins to cherish the beauty that many ignored... he silently plants a kiss and quietly feels the heavenly element that lies in her feet. As he cherished the moment, she whispered something that delivered a whiplash to the riddle that was surrounding them. As he caressed and embraced her feet that showed him signs of the creator's artistic expertise and his own mad love, she told him how more she loved the young morning than the dying night that wished to be hers only... all that was left was sound of dreams breaking one by one like glasses. "He smiled because the night was really beautiful just like her... He cried deep inside because he knew he had to walk back through the broken glasses, only to bleed again in silence" – Immortal Lover ~B

Hopeless

Being a human they say is for a purpose greater than anyone can define in worldly words. We do have a darker side to every aspect that many avoid to see and one of them is living with a hope that you will breathe tomorrow. The truth is we all are dying since the moment we were born with chains that not many can see.

I hope to see you every night lying with me as we listen to the story of the silence,
If I was not so hopeless… may be this silence would never welcome me with tears,
I know if you were not only in my conscience,
I would have told you in real for a change how much I miss your presence in my wasted life,

The voices in my head seem to vanish every now and then,
As if they wish to betray me more often… like life has been doing,
It plays a game with me as if I'm a lost child wandering in search of joy,
Once it has a toy for me and when I run towards it all I see is laughing faces again,

Pointing fingers and pokes that have made me bleed,
It doesn't matter even if it means losing all the red wine I have within me,
I still hope to bring you back in any form,
I hope to cherish lost moments with you before even time betrays me….

Yours forever – Immortal Love ~B

Till eternity

From body to my soul within, I see your marks your wounds bestowed upon me as love. I never knew love could be so kind to me that I would get you as gift to cherish and a memory to carry with me forever. The story of my happiness starts with your smile and it is in your eyes I see my dream dwelling within the care of deep memories of the moments we spent together.

Before we met, I was just alive without even a slight idea of what pain or even pleasure meant. The moment I saw you, I felt a star born within that enlightened my wanderer soul that had lost its will to continue eons ago. Within you I feel the existence of the creator and you are the one who defines the pacifier of good and evil for me.

I may appear to be a stalker as I stare at you while you sleep. Even though my eyes wish to sleep too and they burn while I refuse to even blink, but how can I miss such a wonderful union of heaven and blissful night. To love you has always been my state of worship, for you are my redemption from the immortal pain that I carry since ages.

"She takes a deep stare at me and peeps into the oceans of my eyes that wait to raise havoc,

She says that she doesn't love me,

My angel doesn't even know how to lie a bit…"
– Immortal- Ben

The Mistress

Like a flower that bends in this cool breeze, I wait for her with tears in my drowsy eyes. Million stars burning at the same time and I still wish to see the one that burns my heart. As we walk together I see a godly grace walking with her that makes everything within me come back to life. We already know the journey is not that long as I desire, so let's walk together as much as we can.

She shuns away all the words that my heart creates in admiration of her beauty,

I am yet to learn to live without her and this life seems so short to love her endlessly,

Life does not seem to like my intentions so I decided to die in her arms while the stars guide us to our rightful realm,

It seems fate was already laughing at my dreams and so was my mistress, who still looked beautiful, even when she laughs at my misery,

With you my barren heart got the sky it needed,

With you I was one step closer to the life I dreamed of,

Take this too when you go because without you I have no intentions to live,

Learned you and your beautiful smile my mistress... but I could never learn to live without you...!

Yours forever~ Immortal lover

For a Moment...

For a moment we have found this time that teaches how selfless love can be, For a moment I found life in your beautiful eyes that refuse to stop staring at me, For a moment, I wish to stay and live with you...

I don't know how long this moment will stay with us, For a moment let's push this distance away and cross our hearts, For a moment let me hide within your tense heartbeats, For a moment, I wish to die in your arms and become your immortal lover,

Why do you wish to burn alone, when you have me waiting to embrace you with your pain? I know the pain that comes with each passing breath and I know the numbness that rules your mind, For a moment allow me to take you to my story land, For a moment, allow me to treat you as my mistress and sleep with you through the endless nights....

All these years I was waiting with a sword hanging up my throat, For a moment I saw hope in for of you walking towards me with the sweetest smile, For a moment let me show you the madness that this love possesses only for you, For a moment, allow me to hold your lip within mine as you read my story within the wet aisles that rule my eyes... –Immortal lover–

The Drunk poet

Some say he writes pain while some believe he writes his own stories that reflect the perfect combination of pain and agony together. Million readers with billion perceptions and if you ask him, all he replies with a sick smile is of a legacy that has no lineage. All he wished for is a story that makes the reader cry in pain, for the eyes don't possess the vision to depict a tale inked in blood... an incomplete story of a lover who still waits in the dark, bound by limitless time and a bizarre commandment of nature.

The drunken poet sees what many refuse to see and that is the mask that people are used to wearing now. He believes that we all live in a world of lie, wherein deep inside he still waits for his true healer. One who tears away his stories and throws away his blood covered ink, finally making him sleep on her lap. Some who puts him to sleep for good because even he does not remember the last time when he slept with dreams waiting to incept reality?

Such has been the agony which he hides from the world within his heart and such is the pain that when breaks, he coughs nothing but blood and broken dreams. The lonesome dark aisle where he belongs is covered with memories and nightmares that have finally befriended him. The boulevard of broken dreams invites the poet to get drunk so that he is able to see what normal eyes fail to see, a different dimension where his true story talks to him and eases his pain....

"Many come to ease the pain, But their efforts go in vain, Nobody understands the lover's agony, They think their pain is greater... when all I am left with is hatred and god's irony" – Immortal–

May I?

The silence that you hear is nothing but the lonesome song of the night, Feel the cold breeze that rules the night and all you need to do is call, The silence is too curious for you to talk, May I take you in my arms while you sleep through the night?

Let's take a stroll on the dark streets where I belong, Let's visit the corners where I have always been, It's been ages since anybody gave this lover a visit, My time is still stuck in that loop, May I have the permission to hold your hand while we walk?

Even the ocean waves are covered in silence here, Even they don't wish to talk, Let's explore the silence that hides within the moonlight that burns me, Let's listen the song of the rain that came to soothe me, May I hold your lip within mine while you feel the drops on your cheeks?

The silence in my heart is like a free wind, Let me invite you to take a flight with me, The heartbeat you hear is nothing but a forgotten melody, Let me take you close to me and make you feel what they sing… May I ask you to walk with me for a moment called Forever-

Faulty fate

All of a sudden it seems I lost what I stole from the grips of time, A bond undefined, unique in itself,

All I am left with is some broken dreams and a mask to hide my face, I see pointing fingers but no faces as if it signifies my immortal punishment,

What kind of a life I seek forward to without the one I loved? What kind of a second chance does life has to offer when I have to see the one I love in constant pain?

Every time I hug her I leave a part of my soul for her to keep as a souvenir, I wish to wander aimlessly with you again and be one till eternity,

I wish to alter my stars that foretell my destiny, I don't wish to wait for a fate that has you missing with me,

Even though my heart appeals for a friendship with my own pain I don't wish a life without you, I no longer love myself for life is now a burden that I wish to pass on for the one who care....

Curtailed Romance

The aisle is wet as if it just rained; I walk quietly because I don't wish to ruin the enigma that hides within these silent walls. I walk bare feet so that I can feel the dew slowly caressing my wounded feet and soothe the pain caused due to walking all these years. I am not blessed to feel the breeze on my inert skin as I have to keep walking towards a fate that has nothing for the monotonous world of mine.

The only aspect that makes this walk worthwhile is a felling that she is still with me. Quietly she watches me drench in the rains of sorrow and her voice still wanders within my subconscious mind. May be it will take a little time for me to get over the fact that people eventually leave this paradigm for a better place where dreams are manifestations of reality. On the other side, I know she still waits for me to come to her and complete the story that remains curtailed. I talk to her in my cordial silence, in my strange ways where words have nothing to do. She still sings to me in the silence of my heart, a lullaby that helps me sleep. All I am left with is a spirit that seeks refuge and a wish to never come back if I sleep, as my dreams are too beautiful to be demented by reality.

"Never walk so fast that I remain behind,
Don't walk too slow that you remain behind,
Hold my hand and walk with me towards a moment carved in heaven… Immortal Love"

Voices

Something within me still subsists,
An entity dark, tired and familiar,
Following its hums and the advice that follows,
Walking lifeless with each moment full of fear,
They whisper and they understand,
Trading each emotion with unasked protrusion,
They ask me to leave this part of the stand,
As infatuation someday will end in oblivion,
Voices in my head talk to me about the other side,
They say it's better on that part,
Should leave the things that hold you back they preside,
Should I follow the voices and blind my heart….?
-Immortal- Ben

Voices # 2

People have rules and folks have religion but I have a strange voice that guides me to a path that less prefer to travel. When the night comes calling I find myself covered in a strange faith that seems so familiar, as if we share a bond that is unperturbed from the shackles of slumber, a bond that knows no bondage of time.

Humans fear betrayal, which is why they question their faith when tough times come. The voice in my head loves to hate morality and questions the very own existence of sanity. What does being sane in the head have to do with a person like me? For I have always loved this immortal madness of destroying my own existence for the one I love.

"I still see her and they ask me to take my doses,
Why should I stop seeing her?
The only thing that of her left within me is memories and blood coated roses!"

I see a mad rage in my shadow, an endless wish to burn in silence. I see a wicked smile in my shadow that asks me to stop being myself and let go of the anger that subsides within me. I have locked this madness within me for years, but still I talk to this voice from time to time when I feel alone. People think I am mad when I smile without a reason or utter words to myself that have no real world meaning.

People need mad beings like me too because the world is too big a place to house only the sound ones. I see buzzards guiding me towards oblivion in my dreams, for I had to create a necropolis where no one can disturb my silence again. As I walk, I see the lights of dreams dying, I hear voices crying and I have a taste of blood in my mouth as I walk towards the end of my madness.

This life has never been kind to me, for I suffered a fate that no loyal lover suffers. Spending a moment of love that can last forever has ended my story in a loop that refuses to die. I lost everything to the mocking crowd and all I am left with is the voice in my head that tells me the things I should do to attain inner peace...

Like a leaf on water

I float like a lifeless leaf on water that many find gorgeous as a subject of amusement, a moment that justifies the beauty of nature and the existence of hope. Unlike a leaf that many see, it's actually a never ending wait to fade away. A punishment for the eternal being who wishes to re-unite with its higher self but still is trapped in the illusions of time. I long to unite with the immortal one so that my existence becomes a question that will be long forgotten by those around me. I float towards a destiny that is nothing in itself like avoid that needs to be filled with hope. I pity learners who walk carefully as I seem to be the only one who falls for every broken angel I see. Pity is what the caretaker showers on me as I walk a path covered with poisonous thorns and sad that I still live to see my feet bleed to numbness.

I wish to disappear as I float with an immortal wish to disintegrate, a punishment for being a courtesan who is yet to learn to give up. I see myself as a fallen warrior who is not ready to accept the deluge of defeat and still stands under the mirage of love…

"Leasing Life like a fruit that will soon be rotten, Like any other in her life I too will be forgotten…." B~

Together till the end of time

As we walk towards a better part of the world, a voice inside of me says a silent prayer. I stare at the empty corners with a strange fear of losing you in the end. To a man who has lost everything he ever desired, walking with a dream of his own is nothing less than a miracle made of glass that has to be cared with every step. Somehow the prayer says we will be together till the end of time and this story is just a beginning of a beautiful chapter with limitless Love.

Please hold my hand as I am still a child that fears reality… May be the real world is too big for me so I should hide behind your grace or I should close my eyes with a shy smile as you guide me towards oblivion. When I walk with you even the silence speaks a strange language with every stare full of love and need. I have travelled a long road and covered more than I was supposed to, but this life still despises me as try to reach out to her. May be you are my path to redemption so let me sleep besides you, may be you are what I was searching all my life so let me share my life with you……

"Take my memories and burn them into ashes,

Let me paint us together in my dream,

Before the rain comes again and the color it washes…" –
Immortal B⁓

Heartless

Million times he tried to pen down his agony and all that was left was blank pages covered in blood, pain and misery. Stories walk around him like fallen dead leaves that he likes to cover up his lies with, but the only story that he wishes everyone to see was missing.

She came like a wish in his lifeless moment and no one knows when she actually became his prayer. She taught him to believe and she taught him to be human again. The true meaning of being loved started with her presence and such was the deepness that words had nothing to do by being with them. Time often froze when amidst taunting crowd they talked to each other just with glances and stares. It was something that was meant to be... Yes, this was something that could be named as Immortal Love.

Whenever they gazed at the empty sky, a strange sense of fear gripped his mind whether all of this was nothing but a dream. A moment that will soon dissolve within the aisles of boundless time... and the sand will soon fade away from his hands, irrespective of his conscious grip. Every time when this fear came calling for the lover, she stood in between with a firm kiss on his forehead, telling him that this indeed was a dream that will stay with them forever.

He made her listen to his heartbeat that called out to her, his body now possessed a familiar aroma that made him feel her presence even though when was not around; his eyes were always in constant search for his lover in crowd and even in the darkest isolations that haunted him whenever she was not around. Yes, this was not love but madness that wrote her name all over his soul.

Like every moment has its timeline, this too had to end but in a fashion that could never be accepted as fate. One day he came to know of the ordeal that she had to suffer due to their innocent bond and an immortal wish to be together forever. When he could not find her anymore, he knew something was wrong because unlike life, she was the only one whom he could trust and expect by his side.

The pain that people around bestowed for loving him was too much for her to bear alone. She fought a battle that was never hers alone and without even a hint of a farewell she departed to a kingdom where she belonged. Time came to an absolute halt with every face laughing at him and mocking him for still waiting for someone who has already left for a better demesne. Yes, she ended her life when she realized that she could not be with him and left him with a punishment worse than death... a WAIT!

The actual punishment was not the wait and the absence, but the fact that he could still see her but not touch her. He talked to her but couldn't feel her, while people around thought of him as just another lover who lost his conscience along with his will to live. They asked him to take his prescriptions for depression but, were he depressed? He pleaded not be forced as all he was left with was her memories that still talked to him in this strange lifeless form.

"Why should I destroy her memories when they are harmless? How can I give someone my heart when I am Heartless?"

Song of the Ocean

After a long while I finally got a gift that I could call as mine, a moment that could last forever. My feet deep in pure water and I saw the waves that were waiting for me as if we shared a common pain; an immortal incompleteness that we both wished to portray and share. The waves had their own story to tell and they wanted me to join them as they scream all night for all to listen and yet, many fail to understand their language. On the other hand, they have me who still survives a battle that was lost a long time ago, but still I stand broken for someone to come and push me away. These waves and I share a bond that none living can understand, as we both have many stories hidden beneath a poker face. They scream in pain at night with nobody as a listener, while I prefer to burn slowly in silence because I know I will never have a listener. People come and enjoy the cool breeze that compliments the sanity of its landscape while they fail to understand what the ocean tries to sing. People come to me with a hope to share their pains, but they hardly see the child that cries all day n' night beneath my demented soul.

How badly I wait for that breeze and for that wave that could wash my pain away and purify my soul of all the maligns, which this life has stamped me with... I need somebody to write the legacy of a lover that never died and lived a life that was an immortal wait. I need somebody to whom I could hold onto and listen to the song that these waves sing to me. Someone who could kiss my wet eyes and drink my tears of sorrow with a smile... like I have been doing for years. I wait for a wave that mends my broken soul and heart, takes me with it to a realm where I belong.
"Let's walk forever and vanish towards oblivion,
Come with me to my realm and sleep to the song of the ocean..." – B~

Nightmare

I can't remember the last time when I slept peacefully. To be true, I can't come with a date when I actually slept at night. It all comes to a strange conclusion that some kind of punishment bestowed upon me, a punishment of resting with open eyes. Even I try to shut my eyes close, I can't keep them closed for long as they long to breath unlike any other of my senses. Why can't I sleep at night?

To me it seems like a strange loop wherein I do sleep but it's the same dream again and again, till I break my conscience into broken pieces of my own happiness. An incomplete painting on a glass canvas, a broken lover kneeling down in front of it and to my surprise I precisely remembers both in tears. The incomplete image is of a woman and the one kneeling down has blood in his hands. Was the artist crying because he couldn't complete the art or was he in tears due to the pain he had to undergo in complete the one that remained incomplete.

I try hard to run after the canvas as i wish to feel the wet ink on my cheeks but Is it the destiny that mocks me even in my dreams? The canvas remains beyond my reach and I wish to run more n' more even the loosing breath does not interest me anymore.

"I look for you here and I search for you there,
Immortal love is nothing but just madness,
You're no longer a dream but just a nightmare…" – **B⁓**

They laugh at me

Holding her picture tight close to my chest, I walked in a dream of my own, I saw people smiling at my happiness, Little did I understand the concept of infatuation… little had I known,

We all are here for a purpose, A motive upon us is bestowed, I only believed in the innocence of her beauty, My faith in godliness was restored,

Deep inside you are always present in my prayers, Every drop in my eye has been a gift from you, Loving you more than me was a mistake I made meaningfully, Not even death can separate my soul from you,

I stared at her astounding beauty for days and nights, For sure nobody could deserve her but me, Pain was my destiny to accept, Even the gods are laughing at me :(

–Your's Forever- Immortal lover~B

Phoenix

There is some kind of anger within me, a strange wish to shout out to the sky as it rains fire. Keep shouting till my voice is no more and the fire melts me into an element from which I was born … ashes. This time I don't wish to come back again, atleast with a defective heart that feels for anyone I see. I see barbwires cutting me inch by inch as I try to reach to the hand that wishes to offer me my salvation. A winged counterpart that teases me as I chase it endlessly and finally stop so that I can catch my breath,

I feel helpless in a situation where I cannot sacrifice my own heart for something better. I wish to feel lifeless again as I see smiling masks around, each with a knife of their own waiting to stab me. I paint a canvas that will soon burn with the fire that rains from the sky. It is this fire that shows me the ire of the creator for never walking the path he showed all of us,

I made a mistake as I chose to stay away from the flock and walked a path that none chose to travel. I wish to sleep peacefully and I long for a night that will not haunt me. I pray to my princess of the night to embrace the darkness within me and let me sleep beneath the stars. I wish to sleep forever as this life is nothing but a strange punishment that never seems to end,

Meant to be

Soon you will be gone forever and I will have to move on seeking a different rain to hide my tears. Life will be lifeless again and I will be lost in my own dreams that somehow bring happiness close to me. I have not touched your soul but still there is some warmth that we share when we are together. I feel my heart shouts your name whenever you are next to me…

Why does it seem that someone somewhere created your precious eyes just for me to adore and dream of… even though it hurts, still I wish a perfect world to you after all this is what immortal bond is all about. Let me sink in the ocean of sorrows for I have to explore a world that human conscience fails to understand.

You will always be the fresh morning dew that many await and I will be the dusk that many bid adieus. As I prepare myself for the inevitable departure, a moment where my lifeless dreams burn in silence and my lips smile while my eyes still sing a prayer of hope. A strange wish like a tiny star twinkles inside me that still dreams of starry evening with me lying beside you. While you count the stars and I count the blessings bestowed on you by the creator, let's enjoy this moment of silence.

Take a deep look at the eyes that adore you, take a step closer to me so that the world can know the true meaning of an immortal bond. Forget the smiling masks that mock their own unsolicited venoms and lead a miserable punishment called life.

"Before you go the immortal lover wants you to know,
Spark in your eyes depict something greater than heaven,
Your innocence speak to me as if every sin can be forgiven,
I will wait in the darkest corners of your heart,
Such is the feeling I have for you that even death can never
tear apart...."

You're my Healer

Often I wonder why this life seems so short, or is it the Love that dwells in me makes me feel a miser, who saves each and every breath to spend with the one who waits to heal me. Every day I spend is a new bargain that I snatch from the almighty, a gruesome wait to be granted with a bonus day so that I can spend more time with you my love.

"Because you're the only one who can heal me and offer me salvation from this vicious play, this character that I am tired of playing again n' again."

In your smile I seek power and in your laughter I seek the soulful solitude. It is in your happiness I found hope of redemption because when you look at me for a moment, I turn a careless face towards the mad world that surrounds me. Between your lips I seek a secret to my existence as your immortal lover and in your arms I wish to sleep forever…

"Because you're the only one who has the ability to heal me and I'm tired of this lonesome journey of finding the reason behind my existence…"

Whatever that is left of my life is nothing but an element of your grace, which is why I wish to end the same in your arms, drawing the final breath while staring in your perfect eyes. Your wish is a blessing for me and I still try to uncover the depth of our bond that is yet to be named. No matter how far I wander from you my healer, I will always be there for you when you need me, for I am like no other mortal around you… I am the secret admirer that dwells within the darkest corners of your heart; feeding on your sorrows and living on your beautiful smile.

"Smile my healer, for this world still needs a soul like you. I was just another warrior who had to fade away with the dusk but you will always be the dawn I wait for....

—The Lonesome Warrior who writes better than he speaks—~ Immortal lover B~

Lonesome Warrior and Lovely Traveller

"Why doesn't she smile? Isn't she really beautiful?" I asked my colleague, who was still staring at my sudden statement. Such bold declarations that too from someone who is yet to adjust to his new work environment was something new to digest for my dear friend. To be true even I don't blame his overly surprised looks! They say that I am someone to whom people look up as a source of support when bad times come calling, but then again I am the only one who is still looking for the one who can heal me. At times the pain becomes an obsession to destroy yourself and at times memories leap out of your cage in the form of tears that wish to kiss my lips. "Then, she happened…"

How can silence shout out to the whole world? How can shattered dreams make noise that can force even the maker to bow down? The answer was in her deep eyes that contained an enormous mirage of happiness. The beautiful traveller somehow healed me with her smile and a touch that only I could feel. As we stared at each other, a strange silence ruled my heart… even though the crowd was still ruining my obsession for loneliness. Without even uttering a single word a strange story was being foretold… Story of a 'warrior' who lost his battle of trust and a beautiful 'traveller' who somehow got trapped in the aisles of time.

Where were you my traveller? Was the only question that echoed in my lunatic conscience, because all these days I needed someone who could break the negative barrier and touch my bleeding heart.

"Take my remaining happiness my beautiful Traveller and take my smile,
Hold me close and please walk with me… even if it's for a while…"
– Forever yours,
The warrior of Love B~

The Introvert

"I walk with a million stories by my stride, Sad that I have no listener, Not even a complete dream to cherish with pride,

I see misery in the eyes of those around me, For I hold a mask that smiles, Nobody deserves to see my real face as life still denies me,

They ask me to talk and they ask me to smile, I don't have a heart anymore, Nor do have I a hand to hold even for a while..." – **B~**

-some stories remain incomplete... incomplete forever, Writing these stories is an immortal Lover--

Let's disappear my dear

My soul mate… let's disappear to a nowhere land, where there are no doors and are no people to care about, My dear let's go to the dream we built together, a house and a shelter from all the worldly gallows, Let's disappear my precious…
Allow me to take you to a place where there are no people to mock, Let us wander around a place where are no flock, Take me in your arms for I am tired of the mocking birds that haunt me, Even if it's only a night, I ought to die in your arms… breath last staring in your perfect eyes… Let's disappear my most beautiful poetry…
Please burn the memories that bring pain to us, Let us be one with no space between us, A dip in your soul can purify me my dear, End this pain of loneliness that I can no longer bear,
I only wish this night could stay forever, For you shine more than this moon, Let us dance with you resting on my heart, A heart that whispers your name every time you are near, Let's disappear my only hope…
P.S. – I Love You….

Eyes that wish to sleep

Countless days with all dreams burned, I seek a peaceful sleep that I have actually earned, I don't wish pain and I don't plan love, All I desire is a sleep on clouds up above,

I pray for a peaceful walk on the wet grass, I bid not too much as I am no elegant class, To hold her hand till eternity, It was too much to ask for her eternal sanctity,

I walk a path that leads to nowhere, I stare into extinction that still binds me here, Am I reduced to a liability that is nothing but obsolete? All I know is my vision is all blurry and my eyes wish to sleep...

Enlighten... but let me burn!

Lonesome night, when the wanderers rest for their next flight, there comes an admirer with a heavy heart that wishes to scream. Bending silence to his will, he keeps his heart sealed with the darkest of all the secrets and stories that can stoop reality to his will. He stares at the dim candle that refuses to die against this cruel wind that rules the night. With strain his eye gets wet, but is it the stare that causes his eyes to give up?? Or is it the deep memories that wish to reveal themselves through tears??

Endless wait for queen of the Night to come, as he lies on the dry barren land staring at the stars smiling at him. Each star it seems is telling a story while the sky sings the admirers glory. Wish the dream never ends, for happiness exists here and the real world does not treat the character so well. Deep inside the fire of rejection still burns within him and as he seeks the fountain of love he is deemed to burn day n' night. May be the flames of agony can enlighten those who surround him.... May be he has to burn in order to emerge cold and lifeless. Lifeless so that nobody can hurt him or betray his emotions.

Alone

Million stories that I wish to tell, Billion tales that I have burned, I walk a road that leads to nowhere, Figuring of the life I have lived and the punishment that I have earned, Emotions that flow throughout my body as blood, I preferred not to project them as nobody could care less, I tried to make everyone smile as a clown, In the end they named me a lunatic shameless,

Showing your soft side to anyone could leave you vulnerable, Today nobody cares if you're hurt deep inside, People have a strange habit of scratching old wounds, I still prefer to walk by the aisles alone with pain concealed by my stride,

"Million stories to tell, Billion tales to burn…" – Immortal lover-B

Intangible

My heart remembers you with each incomplete breath, I always knew that I can't have you but still wished to try till death, This is what we call madness and revenge, Funny is the fact that it was never an illegitimate love affair to avenge, Love doesn't hurt for it will always be a substance sacred, It is emotion that people play with and leave the other one with hatred, I ask for justice and I ask for a fair trial, I can't love anyone… for I constantly fear denial,

The life seems so lifeless and ever so dull, I still sleep beneath the stars waiting for a miracle, Deep inside I wish to love again so that I can write a better story, It seems my stars don't wish to shine and my heart has lost its glory,

You will always be the morning ever pleasant, For I am the fading dusk still seeking the past over present, I am the lip that chants the legacy of the lover unbelievable, You will always be in my heart like a prayer intangible…

Immortal Loneliness~ B

The Dream

With magic sprinkled all over as we pretend, We somehow believe that the affair is never going to end, Such is the song of love and hate, You burn in daylight but it's never too late…

Eyes all sleepy with thoughts leaping, Her vision never fades even when I'm not dreaming, When I close my eyes I see us happy & together, An immortal wish of death then rules me forever,

Why life has to be this unfair and to me this hard? Why do I have to fake happiness and smile like a retard? Now I seek happiness and love by making others smile, I end up as a clown with friendships that last only a while……

Confession of an Immortal Lover~ Ben…

Dirty Deeds

Why do people blame love? After all an affair is innocent as a dove, Then why does one scream in the name of lust, When in the end everyone will be reduced to dust,

Biting her lips with an obsession in the dark, We stare at each other with a different pain to lark, In her eyes I saw no need for the madness to go low, Wish the time could stay still as I wanted this to go on really slow,

Let's roll of the floor with our lips locked deep, Let's keep staring at the stars and not sleep, Naked we embrace the warmth of our maligned body, Feeling that drives me insane is rather godly,

"Indulge in this affair as love is what this tangled soul needs, Inevitable as they say... Let's get ready for some dirty deeds..."

Playfully yours,

Immortal- Lover

Lobhaanaa...

I wish to pen about a friend,
But without a titLe there is not much to comprehend,
Her smile studded with stArs was a substance obsolete,
Could light a dying fire with a smile so charming yet incomplete,
To make her laugh for a task ever fascinating,
Like I was under her mystic spell and still recovering,
Sad from the world she seemed depressed,
No matter how lonely I was…but I was impressed,
Lucky is the philanderer who wins her in the end,
Hiding my jealousy with a smile and happiness that I pretend,
Smile dear.. as without your angelic charm the world is a daunted helm,
Will wait for you in afterlife… may be you will smile upon me in other realm…
"Her eyes had a language of their own,
Her incomplete smile was like a pleasant kingdom without a throne"– Please smile for me 'Your Friend'

Need You...?

Why should a heart die alone?

Why should a life lie apart and torn?

Why should a soul be punished so hard?

Why should I be the one walking alone this incomplete boulevard?

Maintained a fruitful bond with darkness,

Until she dragged me into the limelight of devoutness,

Now I find no more darkness as the same friend,

The dark corners have no more an inviting trend,

Such was her touch that even loneliness betrayed me,

Happiness started slithering all over while her charm derailed me,

Only I still see you and nobody,

Still your scent resides within me and it weakens my body,

The world doesn't have words to express hatred I have for you,

To heal me and save myself..... I still Need You!

–Immortal Love~ Ben

Rains

Please rain a little love on me as I seek the monsoons, I seek a climate wherein we both are together, Hiding you from the world I wish to encrypt your name in my barren heart, If love is a rain I wish to feel every drop on my face that forgot how to smile, Have never felt love…so please rain on me, Why is it that my body longs for your warmth? Why my love acts weird when it knows everything? Why is this immortal wait staring at me all the time? Have loved her more than myself then why doesn't it rain on me? Waiting for the love to rain~ Immortal Lover

Fire on Ice

We just met and you still worry betrayal, Instead of romance and acceptance all you have is an innocent denial, Just fell in love and you worry imperfections, Instead of a sweet kiss you plant detached rejections….

It's just an alive morning, I prepare to welcome the mystic light, You still prefer the enigmatic darkness, With inherent denial you always like to fight…

After seas of struggle in bed… I finally see some signs of life, Don't know why you prefer motionless death… why you never wish to be my wife??? May be it's my destiny and maybe it's fate, Lying with you is an immortal lover…then why do you still wait???

It is in your arms I see love, And it is in your embrace I feel alive, Even my beating heart shouts your name, When in my last breath I still strive…

Every curve on the body recites our story, For every possession has a price, May be I was too mad for you in this lifetime, This is why our love will always be like *'Fire on Ice'*….

–Immortal Lover~ Ben

Conceptual Love

Weird was the trade when I asked your pain,
Even an inch of your smile could never go in vain,
May be I loved you a lot,
Bled my heart when I saw you walk alone,
With you I cherished every step …even when the time was
a loan,
May be I trusted you a lot,
Your picture hidden and a smile is all I carry,
Ocean of sorrows inked with your lost memory,
May be I still love you a lot….
A life wasted on love- Immortal Ben

Wish to Sleep

I walk slowly towards a bright end, I am calm and I am frightened, I am alive but I am still numb, The walk never gets over n' all that's left of life is a crumb,

Shallow smiles and hollow masks, Surrounding with monotony is a daunting task, I see fake and feel betrayed, I seek the reaper and like happiness…even death's delayed, Life/ love/ betrayal/ pain is like vicious circle, One never gets out and still life expects miracle, Not within my reach was the light n' life I seek, Now eyes are tired and my soul wishes to sleep………

Immortal Loneliness~ Ben

Follow the Whispers

Closing the door and sealing the stories, Hiding behind the curtain, But still fail to hide my miseries,

She seems scared, still and scattered, May be she fails to hear my heart, Fails to hear the whispers around her withered,

Her eyes seem filled with questions, Why the door is closed? Are there any bad intentions?

With a dim-lit smile I stare at my princess, The door seals this beautiful night that steal dreams, The door confines mischievous air that teases her tress,

Let's dance in the moonlight for my time is brisker, My words are quiet and but my feelings scream, Never believe the rumours but follow the whisper.........

"I wish to sleep but memories still haunt me, I wish to smile but life still forbids me" – B~

The Nightman

The winds blew carelessly that night… a misty dusk for us to pretend,

May be these thoughtless waves were a warning of the endless romance that was about to end,

As expected the Nightman came riding to meet his love,

Hiding behind the shadows of the lover were the guardsmen with shackles hidden beneath their glove,

The time and the path…both were the same,

If only he knew that his love all these years went in vain,

The girl he loved acted as the bait,

Luring him into the unconscious love state,

As he appeared within their reach, there were gun fires and screams,

Finally they caught the Nightman, who had been ruining the state's dreams,

As of the girl, she was nowhere to be found,

Was she guilty of murdering her won love? Or she gave into the spell of the state hound?

Even today some hear the horse galloping down the lane,

Is it some enigma or the lover's soul that still wanders in pain???

–Some stories remain incomplete forever ‖ Writing these stories is an Immortal Lover–

I See You

Gone are the days when sun used to shine on me,
Gone are the winds that bestowed your love upon me,
Gone is your fragrance that defined my existence for you,
Still the sad part is that I See You,
Gone with the wind as they say,
All that was left within me was grief and emotions scattered
like hay,
Defeating all odds and redefining all gods was my love
for you,
But the sad part is still I See You,
Alone in the darkness I wander,
Wearing a mask of a weird joker I spread laughter,
Words can never define the lifetime of pain gifted by you,
But when I close my eyes…I.C.U
Immortal Incompleteness- Ben

Salvation

He cannot live without you,
For you may be the reason for his existence,
You wish to remain anonymous to your beloved,
How strange is this persistence?
He is not able to define this relation,
A bond that refuses to name itself,
Is this the moment that they call 'salvation'?
Why don't they ever reveal themselves?
He gave the desired time,
He gave away the distance,
Still his stars do not shine,
He fails to feel her presence,
To live and die for someone you love,
The affair seems so legit,
Imaginations fail to see the daylight of actuality,
It's better to kill it....
Roaming in search of salvation…..Ben~

Suicidal... I see blood!

Staring at the flawed moon on a lonesome night, I wish to write a story about a lover and his endless fight, Nothing comes to my mind as I realize how demented can be a life, Finally I sat down to write this jinxed story, Lines blazing love & words inked in glory red, I gazed down and all I see is a blank moment where I bled,

Some wounds refuse to heal while some remain afresh, I scratch my own clotted wrist to make it bleed, With this pain I wish to feel human again without any sympathetic heed,

It seems that blood is the perfect ink, To pen a story that still remains an incomplete dream, Wish the readers would cry and after feeling my pain they scream,

Such is the pain that the lover was left with, And a dying heart that was buried in mud, This may be the reason why I feel suicidal and Why I SEE BLOOD..........

Celebrating pain~Ben

Dark Temptations

Walking in a dark room has never been so romantic, The place seems familiar but the moment seems enigmatic, Endless wait for his mistress all charmed up, It is this wild temptation that fills this jagged moment with sweet & timeless magic…

As he moves forward towards the beaming moonlight, His heart fills with joy and every step seems a delight, He finds her eyes in a strange pursuit, With her glares the lover grows mad and his conscience goes kaput…

Where should he hide? Can he even escape? Would he be a profound fool if he resists this beautiful deathscape? Love & Lust now seem to be different sides of the same coin, Does it matter anymore? When the lover has lust growing deep in his groin…

Let them live the moment till the end of time, And take this affair to another paradigm, Maybe the Lover has to burn in silence to enlighten his love, He knows that the pain will always be sweet & the moment sublime…

Never has the lover feared oblivion but the reality often scares him, He wishes to remain hidden with the mistress in the dark as this world disgusts him, They lock their lips deep as words have no virtue anymore, Her sweat gives his face an identity as gracelessness still haunts him…

They embrace each other to an extent called Love Extreme, The lover is also left with a strange fear of everything being just a dream, If it's a dream then let him sleep forever, Immortalize him in her arms and let him sleep with a smile forever~…

By **Immortal Lover~Ben**

Seeking Madness

Even a glimpse of your smile can decimate my pain,
The shine in your eyes when I'm around will never go in vain,
When we're together there will never be a legion of sadness,
All I need to see in your eyes is the same level of madness...
Blindly I no longer seek the shiny star,
Doesn't matter how beautiful they are,
None can ever outshine your vanity and vagueness,
My love for you has always been a step ahead of madness...
The wetness in your lips always leaves me surrounded by nostalgia,
You rarely notice the love in my eyes when you walk besides me,
I still try to shed the image of a dreamer prolonged by sepia...
Why do these feelings still haunt me?
Why do this life pair me with sadness?
As the Child inside me asks, "Is there someone out there who shares my level of Love...My Madness...?"

—**Immortal** Incompleteness~Ben

Will You?

The aisles of life will be darker than ever,
You may see me next to never,
Will you be able to find me?
For years I have been a lonesome traveller,
Wearing a mask and faking a smile forever,
Will you be able to taste my tears?
Often I stumble upon misfortunes,
Falling in love has ended me in deserted dunes,
Will you be able to hold me?
My path has always been inked in blood,
Walking blindly on thorns with face covered in mud,
Will you be able to walk with me?
I may be silent but deep within my heart still cries,
I may lie still and motionless but my broken dream still flies,
Will you be able to hear my silent prayers?
"Never run so fast that you miss me,
Never walk too slow that I miss you,
Just walk with me for a moment called 'Immortal Love'
Forever...."–Ben~

My Precious

I seek the blue moon and I feel the heavenly white star,
Neither of them can eclipse your grace... no matter how
glistening they are,
This mystic light does enlighten the soul, but the inherent
darkness yet so mysterious,
Driven by this madness called love, I wish to dance with you
in this moonlight my precious...
Forget the dance as you shy away from me slowly,
I feel so insecure with your stares and in front of your beauty
I feel so lowly,
Seeking you has always been my destiny,
Missing you has always been an experience so horrendous,
It is then I realized that you were always my precious...
As I hold your hand tight within mine,
An experience that defines life and a touch that's divine,
Your eyes seem so wet as if the stars are about to cry,
I kiss loyalty and a promise to try...
My love can be a poison...mild yet tremendous,
To be or not to be with you is not clear in my destiny,
But you will always be my Precious...
−By your *Immortal lover-*

Life Wasted on Love

Year after year as I grew vary and tired, I feel my nerves wrecked and my heart still wired, Blurry my vision still seemed so hasted, Just realized…on love my life got wasted…
She was my god and she was my pride, To me the definition of love and a to-be bride, With each passing day she grew so beautiful, Never seen a star that could burn someone and yet seem delightful,

Journeyed miles in love and trekked several aisles, Still when the pages flip… I feel confused while penning my tales, Countless cuts and several burns on my heart appear pasted, Just realized…on love my life got wasted…

Timeless Tales from an Immortal Lover-

Frozen Romance

Rarely do we admit how gifted is this life, Until the reaper cometh…with death as its wife, Several moment precious trapped in the isles of sand, What troubles me is the emptiness that wanders my barren land…

Why do thee weep and why do thee cry? Troubling own sacred soul and letting own eyes inertly dry, Time is what waits to mend the heart that is shattered and broken, It is this madness in romance that leaves my soul motionless and Frozen…

Million tales to tell and several memories to burn, Why this romance asks me to live on? When every moment spent without you is like an endless torture earned…

Even the mystic flames fail to purify my soul, A soul which was left by her… bleeding and broken, A glimpse of my eyes will show you the immortal romance… that remains frozen…

Love and Destiny

When the winds touch my heart and cool my soul, It seems as if the world sings my love as listen they all, When I start penning down my heart and my story, It seems all of a sudden the time has stopped and even the earthy words have lost their glory…

The climate seems so dreamy, And the mood seems so weary, As she neared me…I could feel her lips so wet, Her every move that night was written in velvet…

Following her has lead me to a path travelled by less, All of a sudden when I find her close to me…I see my words turn into a dry leaf so lifeless, This life has been a story that begun with her, A sadistic fairy tale that even ends with her…

When my dreams burn in silence… even the smell seems so good, I think I have started enjoying this pain… it seems it was always there in my hood, Some say she was never in my destiny… I will end up embracing pain, But I never believed in the stars… How can they foretell my Story…My destiny and my Pain?

"Every time we met I gave you a rose, I could never find a gift that could match your elegance…"—**Immortal Lover-**

Secret~

Let the wanderer tell you a story, Simple but deep... with each word enchanting a girl's glory... There once was a girl mystically beautiful, Her eyes were spectacled stars while a smile that could leave any human grateful... She was the one... a beautiful mistake that none could regret, Never ask the writer who she was....because it's a lovely Secret...

Unlike the girl... there was a boy, Surrounded by enigma and isolated from earthly joy... He loved his loneliness and he embraced the dark, Violently grating his destiny that only left a painful mark... He saw her smile and forgot the revengeful agony, For a moment it was heaven... as his life and fortune came in harmony...

The girl remained detached and secluded from love, How could she trust a stranger??? After all she was a soft dove... The game of love and hate goes on till eternity, Many a times they defined their bond...

to her it was friendship but to him she will always be an angel re-defining his sanctity... She gave me memories... and a bond never to regret, Please don't ask the writer who she was..........Sshh, it's a secret

Boulevard of Loneliness ~

As I traveled in time and crossed several aisles,
All I was left with were some broken dreams and some shattered tales...
Broken was my life and broken was the reflection,
How could I expect them to stay when there was no conviction...
Gone was the wind and gone were the days,
All that was left were some stories and some endless tales...
I wrote my story with a smile and with happiness to remember for a lifetime,
As I briefed back, all I could see was an empty graveyard with nothing but silence that was divine...
I sat with the book in my hand and started a thoughtless reading,
I saw all my happiness die slowly, like a flower which is every minute fading...
As I was about to cry, it started to rain,
It's difficult to explain the view as the water clogged my eyesight, with all my inked efforts going in vain...
As the sun kissed the sky goodbye,
I could feel the wind and the dead breeze that was about to fly...
As I looked onto the lifeless moon... the light asked me,
Why don't you sing anymore? Why do you still curse me?
How can one sing with a broken heart?
How can one just stand when his life is being torn apart?
Only god knows the depth of this emptiness,
Only I alone travel this boulevard of Immortal loneliness~
-B~

Pick my Poison

Never ending darkness and blood all around is what I see now,

May be it's time to end my life before it gets worse than it is already now.

I see my life full of misery, betrayal and pain,

May be falling in love was a bad deal as my efforts went all in vain.

I see my skin growing pale and my sight growing dim,

May be it's time I leave this cruel paradigm and prolong myself to some other realm.

What did I do with my precious life? Why did it get wasted?

It was foretold that love is a beautiful feeling, never to be hasted.

In my last vision I see every part of my worthless life,

Now I wonder… where did I go wrong? Was it enough to take my own life?

Is it this poison that made me human? Or the pain that it took away for a while,

I came into the world crying, but I always wanted to leave with a smile….

—**Immortal** Confession~Ben

Beautiful death

Times fly and winds blow by as I bid my own farewell to my life…

How can death be as beautiful as it may sound? Breaking the contemporary inclination of being so cruel to the human soul…

I guess the idea of any beautiful death will be of leaving the paradigm with open eyes…

The last vision of the one whom you loved…

For love has gained the image of being immortal…

Carrying on the baton of being a philanderer…I stare into those beautiful eyes…

Little do I realize my breath growing cold and slow…

I get it finally my time has arrived and finally I ran out of time…

Some believe..when it's time, you have your whole life flashing in front of you

However, hardly can I have a same opinion. I saw the moment I couldn't face in my entire life…

It was you… and those lifeless words, which changed my life till perpetuity…

I lay motionless all alone…with a question in my mind…

How could I end up alone?

All those years spent spreading happiness…went in vain when I await my reaper…

Heaven or Hell is not my virtue...I belong to some other dimension, where I can still feel her besides me...

Nor do I care if it is a figment of my imagination...still it will be a delusion to die million times again...

People in love wish to live together...I must be a bizarre lover who wishes to die with you...

By

Immortal Love~*ben*

Lone Wolf

Staring in the mist I see a child,

Perhaps my imaginations have grown a bit wild,

Is it the ecstasy that drives me dawdling,

I believe it's something sort of a gift from life,

Which is yet to become my darling,

Staring me back with enigma in his eyes,

Is a child of my dreams that has always been an element of surprise,

Never the compassion has allowed me to leave,

I believe it's time I accept what past has to retrieve,

The child with a balloon...no smiles...no teary eyes...a situation that stood like a mismatch...

I knelt down to see the past eye to eye...to my surprise I couldn't face the dilemma....

I could see the child filled with disarray...as of why people treated him like an example... a puppet...

Wish I was able to argue him out of the atrocities...but life my friends has always been induced by Darwinism...

I sat with the child as time passed with a pale stare at me... for I was the one breaking the barrier and walking against time...

I sat and I sat...without even a single chat...

I could make out all the sorrowful stories that the child had in his eyes...

Was this a punishment or a revelation...whatever I took by my stride...

I believe the agony of being overshadowed...being misunderstood...being made fun of...

Forsaken by eternity...mislead by destiny...the child still stares at me... at times when I wander like a lone wolf...

By ~*Immortal* Agony *Ben*

Wish I could touch hearts

Why do we wish to see what our eyes wish to see…
Why can't our lives be what it actually should be…Like heaven…
Time's frozen when your soul's not open…
Wish I could touch hearts…wish I could mend hearts…
Why do we blame ourselves for fate and destiny…
When the world is already bleeding in symphony…
What is Hate…what is regret…
Why are we so consumed with love and pain that one should forget…
Wish I could touch hearts…wish I could mend hearts…
Pain n' sufferings destined upon us…
Bedlamites playing the blame game with sufferings bestowed upon…
Constant agony in which I burn…
The infinite fear of losing you…my love…
Wish I could touch hearts…wish I could mend hearts…

Confession of a Lover

You were my chatelaine with a heart of stone, Stones that will be pelt on me every second till my last breath,

Spent a lifetime loving you like a lunatic, looking for every sign that you'll love me back someday,

Things I say, things I show…story written in blood and covered in snow…is a unbosoming …confession of a lover,

All I asked was the feeling of love from you…the imminent… ineluctable… shower to quench my desires for you,

Cold vibes often leave the heart with feelings that don't last a lifetime,

You are the only one capable of hurting my heart…n you played well…with your larger than life part,

Leaving no stones unturned…you gave up to time,

I feel as irresolute…as I write my story and leave to the phenomenon of hatred irrelevant of any dime,

Even rose has a thorn… Venomous enough to lay me down till eternity,

And here I lay on my death bed…those are thorns gifted by you my love,

Will lie down…bid my final goodbyes…to this world, which has not been more than endless chastisement…scratching through my soul and benevolence,

As my heart stops beating…becomes motionless..struck by a poisonous flower,

This my foe is a true 'Confession of a Lover'……

By
~Immortal Pain~ Ben

Storyteller

One misty night…on the darkest hallways, I saw a dark figure arriving towards me,

It was none other than the storyteller who wanders around with his mysterious stories,

Agonizing mystery…the darkest secrets were the storyteller's specialty,

Walking through the lanes of derision. The storyteller has arrived…with him are the voyages he witnessed with love and agony,

With a red rose held firmly bleeding in drops….I see his tears fashioned with a smile,

Leaving behind the memoirs of his love held so tight…a storyteller with a dark past but smile so bright,

I ask him too repeatedly to lend me a story one or many… he smiles back to me with a mirage so many,

Wishing the storyteller to never pass….I loved his smile n I loved his past,

His love waiting for him since eternity…for that is what we call immortal love…Free from the shackles of slavery nor withheld by any boundation,

As I speak of love…Suddenly, I see the storyteller vanishing back….back where he came from the land without a track,

I wait for the story teller to come back again… For there was something me in him,

Rarely did I know… I was staring not at the story teller but my own dreams,

By the time I realized… There was no storyteller and only my dreams,

Thirst of Incompleteness~